Our World Today

An Introduction to Environmental Issues

英語で考えよう！ 地球の未来
クリティカル・シンキングを養う総合英語

Adam Murray　Anderson Passos

NAN'UN-DO

このテキストの音声を無料で視聴（ストリーミング）・ダウンロードできます。自習用音声としてご活用ください。
以下のサイトにアクセスしてテキスト番号で検索してください。

https://nanun-do.com　テキスト番号 [511996]

※ 無線 LAN（WiFi）に接続してのご利用を推奨いたします。
※ 音声ダウンロードは Zip ファイルでの提供になります。
  お使いの機器によっては別途ソフトウェア（アプリケーション）の導入が必要となります。

音声ファイル
無料 DL
のご案内

Our World Today 音声ダウンロードページは
左記の QR コードからもご利用になれます。

About this book

This book was specially designed to teach environmental issues topics to L2 students in a CLIL setting. Although some high-level vocabulary is used, 70% of the words in each main text are inside the first 1000 most commonly used words of English. This allows L2 students to improve their language skills while at the same time learning the content.

The exercises and activities in this book are the result of empirical observation by the authors in their own classes, which makes this book attractive not only from the language point of view but also as a tool for teaching that has been proven to work.

This approach is very effective when used in conjunction with active learning strategies. Critical thinking is promoted in every unit through small group work and by questions that require students to find answers on their own.

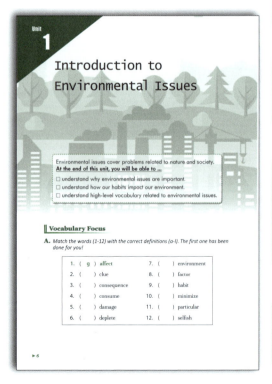

The title of each unit is at the top of the page in large letters.

Every unit has a very appealing and easy to understand picture that gives an idea of what is going to be learned by the students.

A direct caption is present below every unit picture, summarizing the meaning of the unit's title.
Before starting a unit, the objectives are made clear, so students know what to expect.

The matching exercise challenges students on advanced vocabulary that is necessary in order to fully understand the main text.

During the gap-fill activity, students have to, once again, make sure they know all the additional unit vocabulary.

In addition, by having students create their own sentences, instructors can explore vocabulary with different meanings.

At least 70% of the vocabulary used in the main unit texts are within the 1000 most common words of English, helps ensure that even weaker students grasp the content. The work done in Vocabulary Focus makes sure that additional vocabulary is covered before students engage with the unit text.

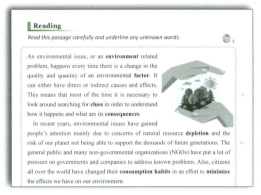

Comprehension of the text is crucial for students to understand the content of the unit. In this part, students are required to go back into the text to find answers. The comprehension section is conveniently placed on the opposite page to make sure that students have access to the text all the time.

To further test students' understanding, this section requires students to fix misleading statements. All information, again, is available in the text on the left page.

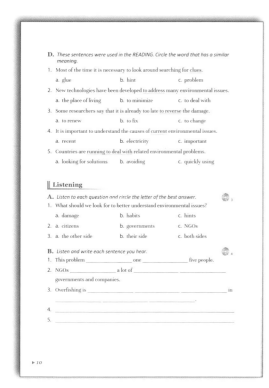

Extra vocabulary work is done by exploring words with meanings that are context dependent.

The questions or the sentences, all commonly related to the topics, are recorded on the audio CD.

Small group discussion can be used to expand the class with student-generated content and promote knowledge sharing among students. Notes and drawings can be made directly in the textbook.

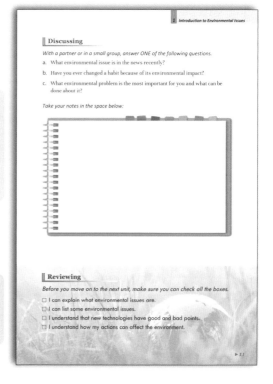

At the end of the unit, students are able to check their learning progress by the use of CAN-DO statements.

Lastly, we would like to make clear that this book does not provide all necessary content to teach a course. Class activities and homework can and should go beyond the scope of this book, but we really hope it will serve as an easy to understand, follow and measure educational tool for both instructors and students.

Adam and Anderson

Contents

1. Introduction to Environmental Issues 6
2. Climate Change 12
3. Energy 18
4. Waste 24
5. Review 1: Units 1–4 30
6. Population Growth 36
7. Pollution 42
8. Water 48
9. Deforestation 54
10. Review 2: Units 6–9 60
11. Hydroelectricity 66
12. Solar Panels 72
13. Wind Turbines 78
14. Nuclear Energy 84
15. Review 3: Units 11–14 90

Unit 1

Introduction to Environmental Issues

Environmental issues cover problems related to nature and society.
At the end of this unit, you will be able to ...

- ☐ understand why environmental issues are important.
- ☐ understand how our habits impact our environment.
- ☐ understand high-level vocabulary related to environmental issues.

Vocabulary Focus

A. *Match the words (1-12) with the correct definitions (a-l). The first one has been done for you!*

1. (g) affect
2. (   ) clue
3. (   ) consequence
4. (   ) consume
5. (   ) damage
6. (   ) deplete
7. (   ) environment
8. (   ) factor
9. (   ) habit
10. (   ) minimize
11. (   ) particular
12. (   ) selfish

a. to reduce something by a large amount so that there is not enough left
b. a thing that you do often and almost without thinking, often something that is hard to stop doing
c. one thing or person among many
d. to use something, to eat or drink
e. a fact or a piece of evidence that helps you discover the answer to a problem
f. the natural world in which people, animals, and plants live
g. **to produce a change on something or someone**
h. physical harm caused to something which makes it less attractive, useful or valuable
i. one of several things that cause or influence something
j. a result of something that has happened
k. caring only about yourself instead of other people
l. to reduce something, especially something bad, to the lowest possible level

B. *Complete the sentences with the words from MATCHING. You may need to change the word form.*

1. Two hundred people lost their homes as a direct _____ of the forest fire.
2. Is there a _____ type of food that she enjoys?
3. Japanese people _____ a lot of rice.
4. It is a good _____ to brush your teeth after eating.
5. He is always _____ and takes the largest piece first.

Writing Sentences

Write two original sentences using words from MATCHING. You may need to change the word form.

1. _____

    _____

2. _____

    _____

Reading

Read this passage carefully and underline any unknown words.

An environmental issue, or an **environmentally** related problem, happens every time there is a change in the quality and quantity of an environmental **factor**. It can either have direct or indirect causes and effects. This means that most of the time it is necessary to look around searching for **clues** in order to understand how it happens and what its **consequences** are.

In recent years, environmental issues have gained people's attention mainly due to concerns of natural resource **depletion** and the risk of our planet not being able to support the demands of future generations. The general public and many non-governmental organizations (NGOs) have put a lot of pressure on governments and companies to address known problems. Also, citizens all over the world have changed their **consumption habits** in an effort to **minimize** the effects we have on our environment.

As countries and businesses run to deal with related environmental problems, time has shown that most changes happen when there is a **particular** interest to be fought for. In most cases, interest groups are quick to show their side of the story to the public. For example, new technologies have been developed in an attempt to address many environmental issues, but little is reported about the side effects and limitations of such technologies or how their use might have even more impact on our environment.

Some researchers say that it is already too late to reverse the **damage** we, human beings, have caused to our planet and that future generations are the ones who will pay for our **selfishness**. Whether it is true or not, it is important for us to not only understand the causes and effects of current environmental issues, but also to make sure that our actions do not negatively **affect** the environment.

(*296 words*)

NOTES non-governmental organizations「非政府組織」

Understanding

A. *Choose the best answer to each question.*

1. To understand environmental issues we have to ...
   a. change the quality and quantity of an environmental factor.
   b. look around to see its consequences.
   c. understand how it happens and its consequences.

2. To minimize the damage on the environment ...
   a. NGOs have put a lot of pressure on governments and companies.
   b. our planet must be able to support the demands of future generations.
   c. people all over the world did not change their consumption habits.

3. New technologies have been developed to address many environmental issues ...
   a. and reports of their side-effects are available.
   b. and these technologies have no impact on the environment.
   c. but little is known about their side effects.

B. *Answer the following questions. Use complete and grammatically correct sentences.*

1. What are environmental issues?

2. Why are people recently getting interested in environmental issues?

3. How can interest groups misdirect our attention to environmental problems?

C. *The following statements have mistakes. Correct them.*

1. Some researchers say that we can still save our planet.

2. The only thing we need to do is to understand the causes of environmental problems.

3. Countries and businesses are showing the public all bad points of new technologies.

D. *These words or phrases were used in the READING. Circle the word that has a similar meaning.*

1. Most of the time it is necessary to look around searching for <u>clues</u>.
   a. glues	b. hints	c. problems	d. questions

2. New technologies have been developed <u>to address</u> many environmental issues.
   a. the place of living	b. to minimize	c. to understand	d. to deal with

3. Some researchers say that it is already too late <u>to reverse</u> the damage.
   a. to renew	b. to fix	c. to change	d. to back up

4. It is important to understand the causes of <u>current</u> environmental issues.
   a. recent	b. electricity	c. important	d. popular

5. Countries are <u>running to deal with</u> environmental problems.
   a. looking for solutions	b. avoiding	c. quickly using	d. handing out

Listening

A. *Listen to each question and circle the letter of the best answer.*

1. What should we look for to better understand environmental issues?
   a. consequences	b. habits	c. hints

2. a. citizens	b. governments	c. NGOs

3. a. the other side	b. their side	c. both sides

B. *Listen and write each sentence you hear.*

1. This problem _____ one _____ five people.

2. NGOs _____ a lot of _____ _____ governments and companies.

3. Overfishing is _____ _____ _____ in _____ _____ _____.

4. _____

5. _____

Discussing

With a partner or in a small group, answer ONE of the following questions.

a. What environmental issue is in the news recently?

b. Have you ever changed a habit because of its environmental impact?

c. What environmental problem is the most important for you and what can be done about it?

Take your notes in the space below:

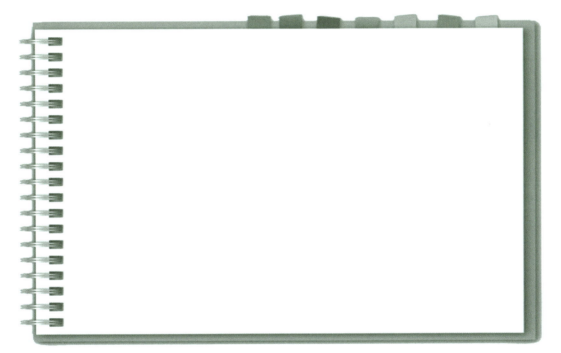

Reviewing

Before you move on to the next unit, make sure you can check all the boxes.

☐ I can explain what environmental issues are.
☐ I can list some environmental issues.
☐ I understand that new technologies have good and bad points.
☐ I understand how my actions can affect our environment.

Unit 2

Climate Change

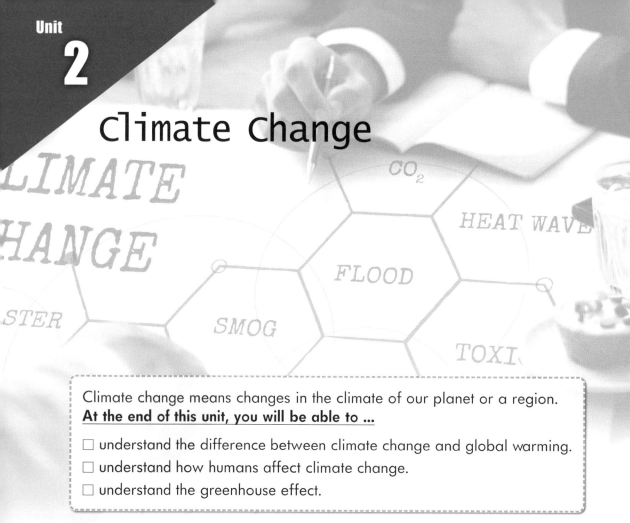

Climate change means changes in the climate of our planet or a region.
At the end of this unit, you will be able to ...

☐ understand the difference between climate change and global warming.
☐ understand how humans affect climate change.
☐ understand the greenhouse effect.

Vocabulary Focus

A. Match the words (1-12) with the correct definitions (a-l). The first one has been done for you!

1. (h) advocate
2. (   ) alleviate
3. (   ) atmosphere
4. (   ) catch-all
5. (   ) enormous
6. (   ) equilibrium
7. (   ) occur
8. (   ) phenomenon
9. (   ) predict
10. (   ) release
11. (   ) skepticism
12. (   ) transportation

a. a fact or an event in nature or society, especially one that is not completely understood
b. knowing in advance that something will happen or what it will be like
c. including several different things without stating clearly what is included or not
d. very large
e. an attitude of not believing statements are true or that something will happen
f. the mixture of gases that surrounds the earth
g. to stop holding something
h. **to support something publicly**
i. a system for carrying people or goods from one place to another using vehicles, roads, etc.
j. a state of balance, especially between opposite forces or influences
k. to happen
l. to make something less severe or painful

B. *Complete the sentences with the words from MATCHING. You may need to change the word form.*

1. Plastic _____ dangerous chemicals when it is burned.
2. The millionaire lives in a(n) _____ house by the ocean.
3. There is a high chance the same problem will _____ again.
4. Experts have noticed changes in the planet's _____.
5. The group does not _____ the use of fossil fuels.

Writing Sentences

Write two original sentences using words from MATCHING. You may need to change the word form.

1. _____

2. _____

Reading

Read this passage carefully and underline any unknown words.

Everywhere around us, we see signs that climate patterns are changing. For example, temperature and rainfall patterns are no longer as **predictable** as in the past. In addition, extreme weather events such as floods and hurricanes seem to be **occurring** much more frequently than in the past. The media often use the term "climate change" and "global warming" as if they are the same. The term "global warming" is specific to temperature rise on the surface of our planet, while "climate change" can be used as a **catch-all** term to describe any climate changes in our planet or a specific region that are the result of additional greenhouse gases in our **atmosphere**.

Greenhouse gases are gases that trap the heat that would otherwise bounce back to space in a **phenomenon** called the greenhouse effect. This mechanism is necessary in order to maintain our planet's temperature and to support life. In recent years, there is a growing amount of evidence showing that climate change is being caused by human activities, which **release enormous** quantities of greenhouse gases into the atmosphere. For example, gases are released during a number of activities such as electricity generation, land use changes, agriculture, and **transportation**.

Unfortunately, these additional greenhouse gases are breaking our planet's **equilibrium** as increased greenhouse gases enhance the greenhouse effect – preventing heat from escaping the atmosphere into space. This in turn contributes to climate changes such as increased temperatures and unpredictable weather patterns.

What can be done to **alleviate** this growing problem? Some people **advocate** for the use of alternative and greener sources of energy like solar and wind. Still, technical limitations, technology maturity and **skepticism** are some of the problems companies and governments face when looking for alternative sources of energy.

(289 words)

NOTES climate change「気候変動」／ global warming「地球温暖化」／ greenhouse gas「温室効果ガス」

2 Climate Change

Understanding

A. *Choose the best answer to each question.*

1. The term climate change ...
   a. contributes to increased temperatures.
   b. describes any climate changes on our planet.
   c. is specific to temperature rise on the surface of our planet.

2. Additional greenhouse gases in our atmosphere ...
   a. can cause climate change.
   b. can help agriculture and transportation.
   c. can support life in our planet.

3. Alternative and greener sources of energy ...
   a. are supported by everyone.
   b. contribute to climate change.
   c. have some people's support.

B. *Answer the following questions. Use complete and grammatically correct sentences.*

1. List some signs that climate is changing in our planet.

2. Why is the "greenhouse" effect important?

3. How can we alleviate climate change?

C. *The following statements have mistakes. Correct them.*

1. "Climate change" refers to global warming.

2. The greenhouse effect is very dangerous and we do not need it at all.

3. Nobody advocates for alternative sources of energy.

D. *These words or phrases were used in the READING. Circle the word that has a similar meaning.*

1. Temperature and rainfall patterns are no longer predictable.
   a. easy to guess   b. easy to do   c. easy to find   d. easy to clean

2. The media use the term "climate change" a lot.
   a. CDs   b. DVDs   c. videos   d. newspapers

3. Some people advocate for the use of alternative and greener sources of energy.
   a. support   b. dislike   c. discourage   d. complain about

4. The term "climate change" is a catch-all term.
   a. important   b. intermediate   c. generic   d. traditional

5. Hurricanes seem to be occurring much more frequently than in the past.
   a. showing   b. predicted   c. reported   d. happening

Listening

A. *Listen to each question and circle the letter of the best answer.*

1. Which one is a green source of energy?
   a. gasoline   b. coal   c. solar

2. a. climate change   b. global warming   c. atmosphere

3. a. unpredictable weather patterns   b. temperature rise
   c. green sources of energy

B. *Listen and write each sentence you hear.*

1. The audience was disappointed by the movie's _____ ending.

2. We hope that the new medicine will _____ the symptoms of the disease.

3. The greenhouse effect is a _____ _____ _____ _____ _____ _____ _____ .

4. _____

5. _____

2 Climate Change

Discussing

With a partner or in a small group, answer ONE of the following questions.

a. What is the difference between "climate change" and "global warming"?

b. In your own words, explain the greenhouse effect.

c. How can new sources of energy minimize climate change?

Take your notes in the space below:

Reviewing

Before you move on to the next unit, make sure you can check all the boxes.

- ☐ I can explain what climate change is.
- ☐ I can list some causes of climate change.
- ☐ I understand the impacts of climate change.
- ☐ I know at least one way to minimize the effects climate change has on our environment.

Unit 3

Energy

Energy is the power required to provide light, heat and to move machines.
At the end of this unit, you will be able to ...

☐ understand the main sources of energy.
☐ understand how humans are dependent on energy.
☐ understand how energy production affects our environment.

Vocabulary Focus

A. Match the words (1-12) with the correct definitions (a-l). The first one has been done for you!

1. (d) cautious			7. ( ) intercept	
2. ( ) destructive			8. ( ) overlook	
3. ( ) emission			9. ( ) power plant	
4. ( ) fossil fuel			10. ( ) renewable	
5. ( ) hazardous			11. ( ) reserve	
6. ( ) impact			12. ( ) sustainable	

a. able to be replaced by nature
b. causing a very large amount of damage
c. to not pay attention to something
d. **being careful about what you say or do, especially to avoid danger or mistakes**
e. to prevent someone/something from arriving at a place
f. the production or sending out of light, heat, gas, etc.
g. a building or group of buildings where electricity is produced
h. fuel such as coal or oil that was formed from the remains of animals or plants
i. a supply of something that is stored so that it can be used at a later time
j. involving risk or danger, especially to a person's health or safety
k. the powerful effect that something has on somebody/something
l. can continue or be continued for a long time without harming the environment

B. *Complete the sentences with the words from MATCHING. You may need to change the word form.*

1. The new player had a positive _____ on the team.
2. The _____ woman rarely rushed to make important decisions.
3. Many household cleaning products contain _____ chemicals.
4. Renewable energy sources are the key to a _____ future.
5. The company had a large cash _____ for times of crisis.

Writing Sentences

Write two original sentences using words from MATCHING. You may need to change the word form.

1. _____

   _____

2. _____

   _____

Reading

Read this passage carefully and underline any unknown words.

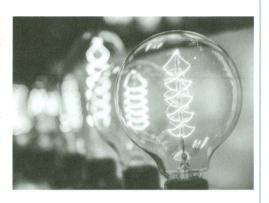

How would our lives be without cars, television, radio, cellphones or even hot water to take baths? Many things are taken for granted by today's generation, but energy and energy production have a great **impact** on our environment. In most countries, the burning of **fossil fuels** such as oil and coal produces the majority of energy. Such a method pollutes our atmosphere and releases greenhouse gases that, as we learned in Unit 2, are one of the factors responsible for climate change.

The demand for cleaner, **renewable** and **sustainable** energy systems started to gain some attention lately, but even clean energy sources can affect our environment negatively. One example is the use of hydrogen in cars instead of gasoline. Such change guarantees zero **emission** of carbon dioxide (CO_2) in the atmosphere, which is great for the environment, but energy is still necessary to produce hydrogen from water. If that energy comes from unclean sources, then hydrogen is not really a solution to the problem. Another example is the use of solar panels to generate electricity. We can say that solar panels offer a clean way to produce energy only if we **overlook** the facts that many batteries are required to store the energy and that the commercially available solar panels release extremely **hazardous** toxic gases when recycled.

As we can see, energy is a very important environmental issue. If we do not change our habits, we might even deplete our natural fossil fuel **reserves** one day. However, we still need to be **cautious** about changing habits without proper planning because the solution might be even more **destructive** to the environment.

(270 words)

NOTES hydrogen「水素」／ carbon dioxide (CO_2)「二酸化炭素」

Understanding

A. *Choose the best answer to each question.*

1. In how many countries are fossil fuels used to produce energy?
   a. all
   b. most
   c. some

2. What is a negative impact of burning fossil fuels?
   a. greenhouse gases are released
   b. hydrogen is produced
   c. toxic gases are recycled

3. Recently, there is a demand for what?
   a. renewable and hazardous energy
   b. renewable and reliable energy
   c. renewable and sustainable energy

B. *Answer the following questions. Use complete and grammatically correct sentences.*

1. How does our need for energy impact the environment?

2. Why should we be skeptical about new energy solutions?

3. How can we minimize the effects of energy production on our environment?

C. *The following statements have mistakes. Correct them.*

1. The burning of fossil fuels is not responsible for climate change.

2. Cars that use hydrogen instead of gasoline are 100% clean.

3. Changing our habits is more damaging to the environment.

D. *These words or phrases were used in the READING. Circle the word that has a similar meaning.*

1. Many things are <u>taken for granted</u> by today's generation.
   a. sometimes available for
   b. sometimes not available for
   c. not available for
   d. always available for

2. The <u>demand</u> for cleaner energy systems started to gain some attention lately.
   a. search
   b. order
   c. request
   d. proposal

3. Such change <u>guarantees</u> zero emission of carbon dioxide in the atmosphere.
   a. prevents
   b. ensures
   c. encourages
   d. prohibits

4. Solar panels are green only if we <u>overlook</u> the fact that many batteries are required to store the energy.
   a. want
   b. request
   c. suspend
   d. ignore

5. We might even deplete our natural fossil fuel <u>reserves</u>.
   a. place
   b. energy
   c. stock
   d. situation

Listening

A. *Listen to each question and circle the letter of the best answer.*

1. Where can hydrogen be used instead of gasoline?
   a. automobiles
   b. factories
   c. houses

2. a. all the time
   b. when clean sources are used
   c. when non-clean sources are used

3. a. a few
   b. some
   c. many

B. *Listen and write each sentence you hear.*

1. All energy _____ have some _____ on our environment.

2. Some people _____ that you can never be too _____ while driving.

3. Hydropower plants _____ water flow and _____ mechanical _____ into electricity.

4. _____

5. _____

3 Energy

Discussing

With a partner or in a small group, answer ONE of the following questions.

a. What is the main source of energy in your country?

b. What would be the biggest impact in your life if there were no electricity for one day?

c. How can you help minimize the impact of energy production on our environment?

Take your notes in the space below:

Reviewing

Before you move on to the next unit, make sure you can check all the boxes.

☐ I can explain the importance of energy production.
☐ I understand the advantages and problems of clean energy.
☐ I understand the impacts of energy production on our environment.
☐ I know at least one way to reduce the impact of energy production.

Unit 4

Waste

Waste is anything that cannot be used or is not wanted anymore.
At the end of this unit, you will be able to ...

☐ understand how waste impacts our environment.
☐ understand ways to minimize waste.
☐ understand high-level vocabulary related to waste.

Vocabulary Focus

A. Match the words (1-12) with the correct definitions (a-l). The first one has been done for you!

1. (j) ash
2. (   ) decompose
3. (   ) flammable
4. (   ) groundwater
5. (   ) ignite
6. (   ) incinerate
7. (   ) landfill
8. (   ) refurbish
9. (   ) rough
10. (   ) soil
11. (   ) toxic
12. (   ) waste

a. to use more of something than is necessary or useful
b. to clean and decorate a room, building, etc. in order to make it more attractive, more useful, etc.
c. not exact; not including all information
d. to be destroyed slowly by natural chemical processes
e. poisonous; having poison
f. the top layer of the earth in which plants, trees, etc. grow
g. water that is found under the ground in soil, rocks, etc.
h. an area of land where large amounts of waste material are buried
i. to start to burn; to make something start to burn
j. **the grey or black powder that is left after something has been burnt**
k. to burn something until it is completely destroyed; burn to ashes
l. something that can burn easily

B. *Complete the sentences with the words from MATCHING. You may need to change the word form.*

1. Gasoline is a _____ liquid obtained from petroleum.
2. Teenagers often _____ money buying clothes they don't really need.
3. The popular shop sells a lot of excellent _____ furniture.
4. We have to _____ the amount of CO_2 released into the atmosphere.
5. We need a lighter to _____ the charcoal before starting the barbecue.

Writing Sentences

Write two original sentences using words from MATCHING. You may need to change the word form.

1. _____

_____

2. _____

_____

Reading

Read this passage carefully and underline any unknown words.

Most activities performed by us generate trash or **waste**. Waste is any material that cannot be used or is no longer wanted. As an example, the United States alone produced about 254 million tons of trash in 2013, **roughly** 2 kilograms a day for every citizen. That is a lot of trash. All over the world, some of the trash we generate is recycled or recovered, but most of it ends up in **landfills** or is **incinerated**, raising new concerns about its impact on our environment.

Landfills have been used long before recycling became popular. At a landfill, waste collected by trash companies is dumped into specific areas, compacted and then covered with **soil**. One of the biggest problems with landfills is the contamination of land and water. The mixture of chemicals coming from the many products buried there can produce **toxic** gases and even be washed away into the water supply. Additionally, indirect fires might **ignite** due to the presence of methane, a highly **flammable** gas that results from the **decomposition** of organic matter.

Burning waste is an easy way to get rid of it, but some waste can release toxic gases when burnt, which contribute to additional environmental problems. For example, toxic substances are released into the air, soil, and **groundwater** by the smoke and **ashes**. However, burning waste can be used to generate energy. Some people advocate that more energy can be saved by reusing materials instead of destroying them. However, others say that burning waste may be a solution to our energy problems and it could also help in our fight against climate change since the CO_2 emissions are about half compared to landfills.

For now, one thing we all can do is to try to reduce the amount of waste that we produce. In recent years, the idea of Reduce, Reuse, Recycle (or the 3Rs) became well known worldwide, but some environmental groups are pushing for many other "R"s like Refuse, Repurpose and **Refurbish**. Even if we cannot see eye to eye which Rs are important, we can all agree that waste is a problem that needs more attention.

(354 words)

NOTES US ton=907.185kg／contamination「汚染」／methane「メタン」／Refuse「辞退」／Repurpose「転用」／Refurbish「改装」

4 Waste

Understanding

A. *Choose the best answer to each question.*

1. Some people advocate for the burning of waste instead of using landfills because …
   a. it can be used to generate energy.
   b. it contaminates groundwater.
   c. it is an easy way to get rid of it.

2. We can help the environment by …
   a. burning our waste to get rid of it.
   b. collecting waste and using more landfills.
   c. reducing the amount of waste we produce.

3. Methane is not a gas that …
   a. is highly flammable.
   b. results from decomposition of organic matter.
   c. is used to burn waste.

B. *Answer the following questions. Use complete and grammatically correct sentences.*

1. What happens to the trash we produce?

2. How can waste affect our environment?

3. What other "R" would you create? Write down the meaning of it.

C. *The following statements have mistakes. Correct them.*

1. Every one of us produces 2 kilograms of waste a day.

2. Landfills became popular after recycling became well known.

3. Incinerating waste is the best way to get rid of it.

D. *These words or phrases were used in the READING. Circle the word that has a similar meaning.*

1. Most trash ends up in landfills or is incinerated.
   a. buried   b. burned   c. washed   d. dug

2. Indirect fires might ignite because of methane.
   a. stop burning   b. continue burning   c. start burning   d. prevent burning

3. One of the biggest problems with landfills is the contamination of land.
   a. poisoning   b. elimination   c. purification   d. sterilization

4. Let's try to reduce the amount of waste that we produce.
   a. number   b. a lot   c. a few   d. quantity

5. The mixture of chemicals can produce toxic gases.
   a. create   b. burn   c. contaminate   d. eliminate

Listening

A. *Listen to each question and circle the letter of the best answer.* 🔘 12

1. What happens to most of the trash we generate?
   a. it ends up in landfills or it is burned   b. it is recycled or recovered
   c. it is refurbished

2. a. contamination of land   b. generate energy   c. toxic gases

3. a. recycling   b. more attention   c. to become more popular

B. *Listen and write each sentence you hear.* 🔘 13

1. The police officer found a _____ body near the river.

2. The _____ near the old factory was very _____.

3. Some plants grow very well _____ _____ _____.

4. _____

5. _____

Discussing

With a partner or in a small group, answer ONE of the following questions.

a. How much trash do you produce in your house?
b. Have you ever bought a second-hand (used) product?
c. Do you know of a place that was built on a landfill?

Take your notes in the space below:

Reviewing

Before you move on to the next unit, make sure you can check all the boxes.

☐ I can explain why waste is an environmental issue.
☐ I can list some sources of waste.
☐ I understand the impacts of waste on our environment.
☐ I know at least one way to reduce the impact of waste.

Unit 5

Review 1: Units 1–4

Part 1: Photographs

You will hear four short statements. Look at the picture and choose the statement that best describes what you see in the picture.

1.

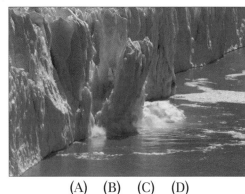

(A) (B) (C) (D)

3.

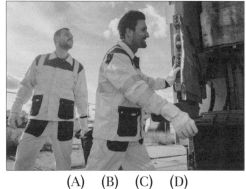

(A) (B) (C) (D)

2.

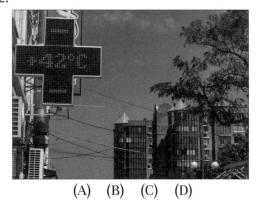

(A) (B) (C) (D)

4.

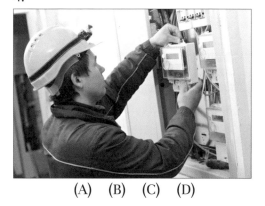

(A) (B) (C) (D)

Part 2: Question-Response

You will hear a question or statement followed by three responses. Choose the best response.

1. (A) (B) (C)
2. (A) (B) (C)
3. (A) (B) (C)

4. (A) (B) (C)
5. (A) (B) (C)
6. (A) (B) (C)

Part 3: Conversations

You will hear short conversations. Questions 1-3 refer to the first conversation and Questions 4-6 refer to the second conversation. Choose the best answer to each of the three questions.

1. Who most likely are the speakers?
   (A) Coworkers
   (B) Researchers
   (C) Weather forecasters
   (D) Students

2. What are they talking about?
   (A) The cooler
   (B) The game
   (C) The weather
   (D) The time

3. Why has forecasting become more difficult?
   (A) Patterns are changing.
   (B) Patterns are confusing.
   (C) Patterns are constant.
   (D) The weatherman is not precise.

4. Where is this conversation most likely taking place?
   (A) A home
   (B) A library
   (C) A supermarket
   (D) An office

5. What are they likely doing?
   (A) Cooking
   (B) Studying
   (C) Watching TV
   (D) Drinking with friends

6. What is the man likely to do next?
   (A) Check the number
   (B) Recycle the thing
   (C) Throw it outside
   (D) Put it in a bin

Part 4: Talks

You will hear a short announcement. Choose the best answer to each of the three questions.

1. Who is hosting the event?
   (A) A business organization
   (B) A dairy
   (C) The city hall
   (D) The school board

2. When is the event?
   (A) April 9th
   (B) April 13th
   (C) October 9th
   (D) October 13th

3. Who is the event intended for?
   (A) Business people
   (B) Government employees
   (C) High school students
   (D) Scientists

Part 5: Incomplete Sentences

A word is missing in each of the sentences below. Choose the best answer to complete each sentence.

1. The developers are unsure what the ------- of the project will be.
    (A) advocate
    (B) affect
    (C) effect
    (D) phenomenon

2. Although the doctors cannot eliminate her problem, they can ------- her pain.
    (A) alleviate
    (B) avoid
    (C) decompose
    (D) refurbish

3. The ------- child did not share her toys with her sister.
    (A) cautious
    (B) destructive
    (C) predictable
    (D) selfish

4. The careless man did not think about the ------- of his actions.
    (A) atmosphere
    (B) consequences
    (C) equilibrium
    (D) transportation

5. It is sometimes good to be ------- of things we are told.
    (A) destructive
    (B) predictable
    (C) renewable
    (D) skeptical

5 Review 1: Units 1–4

Part 6: Text Completion

Four words are missing in the text. Choose the best answers to complete the text.

Future Technology's Smart Home System is the perfect way to ------- your home!
1.
What exactly is the Smart Home system? It is a system that allows you to -------
2.
many of the systems and to control the electronic devices throughout your home with a remote control or even your smartphone!

You may be surprised to learn that your home already has systems that can be automated. For example, heating and cooling systems, security alarms, lights, and kitchen appliances. In no time at all, your devices can be connected to the Smart Home System.

Naturally, there are a number of benefits from having the Future Technology Smart Home System installed in your home. For many people, security is a concern. The Smart Home System application (Smart Home on the Go) gives you the ability to check whether or not your doors are locked, to watch the video feeds from your security cameras, and to even turn on and off the lights—even if you are out of town! Secondly, and most -------, the Smart Home System makes your home
3.
more energy efficient. For example, the heating or cooling systems can be turned off when nobody is home and turned back on an hour before everyone returns. Also, blinds and curtains can be opened and closed to take ------- of the weather.
4.
Are you interested in learning more about the Smart Home System? Call our award-winning customer service at 1-800-SMART-HOME (1-800-7678-4663) to learn more.

1. (A) develop
   (B) eliminate
   (C) modernize
   (D) restore

2. (A) automate
   (B) install
   (C) turn
   (D) update

3. (A) automatically
   (B) importantly
   (C) interestingly
   (D) understandingly

4. (A) advantage
   (B) coverage
   (C) disadvantage
   (D) powerage

Part 7: Reading Comprehension

Read the article followed by four questions. Choose the best answer to each question.

ANDERSON COUNTY
ALL-IN-ONE RECYCLING

Paper—Cardboard boxes (cereal boxes, pizza boxes, tissue boxes, paper towel and toilet paper tubes), catalogues and magazines, newspapers and flyers, letters, envelopes (remove the plastic window first), greeting cards, brochures, non-foil gift wrap, paper bags, telephone books and paperback books, soup and beverage cartons.

 Plastic—Clean plastic jugs, bottles, packaging and non-bottles with the recycling symbols 1, 2, 4, and 5. Do not recycle plastics with 3, 6, and 7 symbols. Medication bottles cannot be recycled. Do not recycle foam cups, food containers or packages.

Metal—Aluminum and steel cans, metal jar lids, steel bottle caps. Containers must be empty.

 Glass—Glass bottles and jars (lids must be removed). Bottles and jars must be empty.

IMPORTANT INFORMATION
No liquids
No garbage
No food residue
No windows
No mirrors
No e-waste (batteries, electronics, etc.)

Only recyclables that are inside Anderson County Blue Boxes will be picked up. Anything outside the collection containers will be picked up as garbage. If you need more information, please contact us at 903-268-CITY (2489).

5 Review 1: Units 1–4

1. Where is this text likely to be found?
    (A) A business magazine
    (B) A catalogue
    (C) A newspaper
    (D) An encyclopedia

2. Which of the following is true?
    (A) All plastics can be recycled.
    (B) Most plastics can be recycled.
    (C) No plastics can be recycled.
    (D) Some plastics can be recycled.

3. Which of the following CANNOT be recycled?
    (A) Electronic dictionaries
    (B) Hardcover books
    (C) Magazines
    (D) Telephone books

4. What will happen to materials not placed in Blue Boxes?
    (A) They will also be recycled.
    (B) They will be put away.
    (C) They will become trash.
    (D) They will not be picked up.

Unit 6

Population Growth

Population growth is an important issue because more people on the planet means more resources are needed.
At the end of this unit, you will be able to ...

☐ understand how population growth affects our environment.
☐ come up with suggestions to population growth.
☐ understand high-level vocabulary related to population growth.

Vocabulary Focus

A. Match the words (1-12) with the correct definitions (a-l). The first one has been done for you!

1. (g) address
2. (   ) birth control
3. (   ) collective
4. (   ) contraception
5. (   ) empower
6. (   ) estimate
7. (   ) fertility
8. (   ) livestock
9. (   ) lust
10. (   ) migrate
11. (   ) prejudice
12. (   ) racism

a. to move from one place to another
b. to imprecisely calculate the number, value, etc. of something
c. the animals kept on a farm, for example cows or sheep
d. very strong desire for something or enjoyment of something
e. to give somebody the power or authority to do something
f. the practice of controlling the number of children a person has, using various methods of contraception
g. **to give attention to or deal with a matter or problem**
h. the practice of preventing a woman from becoming pregnant; the methods of doing this
i. dislike for a person based on their race, religion, sex, etc.
j. done or shared by all members of a group of people; involving a whole group or society
k. unfair treatment of people who belong to a different race
l. the ability to have children

B. *Complete the sentences with the words from MATCHING. You may need to change the word form.*

1. We _____ decided that men and women are equal.
2. I can give you a rough _____ of the amount of wood you will need.
3. The _____ landlord would not rent apartments to foreigners.
4. The farmer needed a new truck to transport his _____.
5. There are many ways to _____ this issue.

Writing Sentences

Write two original sentences using words from MATCHING. You may need to change the word form.

1. _____

2. _____

Reading

Read this passage carefully and underline any unknown words.

The world's population or population growth is seen by many as one of the main environmental issues we are facing due to the **collective** demand we put on our planet. Experts **estimate** that our planet's population will reach 8 billion by 2050, and many environmentalists are considering a range of environmental problems as a direct consequence of this.

As more people are born, our planet's forests, oceans, and lands are impacted. More lumber is extracted for timber, more fish and oxygen is consumed and more land is needed to grow food, raise **livestock** and for building houses and roads. Also, people in developed countries have higher standards of living with high consumption lifestyles and purchasing habits that are often driven by **lust** instead of necessity, making an even greater strain on resources.

As with other environmental issues, many solutions have been suggested to manage population growth. **Empowering** families to plan the number of children is a widely accepted solution that governments can implement, especially in developing and least developed countries. Providing family planning services and accurate information on **contraceptives** and reproductive healthcare is essential for families who would prefer to delay having children.

Education and creation of job opportunities for women is seen as another significant way to **address** population growth. Women who are educated are likely to delay marriage and, consequently, giving birth. This helps to ensure that the children will grow in an environment that is suitable for them, with parents who are more likely mature and in a favorable economic situation. As a side effect, it also helps us to address poverty, as educated people tend to have smaller families.

Discussing population growth is a very difficult and delicate topic. Many developing countries have higher birth rates and most of the world's population lives in poor countries, so pushing for **birth control** might lead to **prejudice**, and discouraging **migration** may lead to **racism**. In addition, most religions favor **fertility** over contraception methods, complicating this discussion even more.　　　　(*330 words*)

NOTES

developed countries「先進国」／ developing countries「開発途上国」／ least developed countries「後発開発途上国」（開発途上国の中でも特に開発が遅れている国）／ family planning「家族計画」／ reproductive healthcare「リプロダクティブヘルス（性と生殖に関する健康）」／ birth rate「出生率」

Understanding

A. *Choose the best answer to each question.*

1. More people living on our planet means that ...
   a. we have more solutions to this problem.
   b. we use more natural resources.
   c. we will soon be without space.

2. Women who are educated usually ...
   a. get married faster.
   b. get married later.
   c. get married many times.

3. Education helps us to address poverty because ...
   a. educated people get better jobs.
   b. educated people have more money.
   c. educated people have fewer children.

B. *Answer the following questions. Use complete and grammatically correct sentences.*

1. Describe how population growth affects our planet.

2. What other environmental issues do you see related to population growth? Why?

3. How can education help to address population growth?

C. *The following statements have mistakes. Correct them.*

1. Creating jobs that pay better is seen as a solution to poverty.

2. People in developed countries buy only what they need.

3. Many people don't think population growth is a problem.

D. *These words or phrases were used in the READING. Circle the word that has a similar meaning.*

1. World population is a main environmental issue we are facing.
   a. ignoring   b. overlooking   c. looking for   d. dealing with

2. In developed countries, people's purchasing habits are often driven by lust.
   a. strong desire   b. love   c. hunger   d. hate

3. Empowering families to plan the number of children is a widely accepted solution.
   a. licensing   b. preventing   c. enabling   d. providing

4. Pushing for birth control might lead to prejudice.
   a. opening   b. advocating   c. talking   d. studying

5. As more people are born, more fish and oxygen are consumed.
   a. burned   b. needed   c. produced   d. used

Listening

A. *Listen to each question and circle the letter of the best answer.* 19

1. Why is population growth an environmental issue?
   a. more resources are needed   b. it helps family planning
   c. it is an accepted solution

2. a. education   b. discouraging migration   c. creating job opportunities

3. a. creation of job opportunities   b. more fish is consumed
   c. more land is used

B. *Listen and write each sentence you hear.* 20

1. Population growth is a very delicate _____ for some people.
2. Our grading _____ still need to be _____.
3. _____ _____ have strict _____ _____ while others have none.
4. _____
5. _____

Discussing

With a partner or in a small group, answer ONE of the following questions.

a. Compare your country's population to another country's population.

b. What do you think can be done to slow down global population growth?

c. If population growth cannot be avoided, what other alternative can you suggest to minimize its impact on our environment?

Take your notes in the space below:

Reviewing

Before you move on to the next unit, make sure you can check all the boxes.

- ☐ I can explain why population growth is an environmental issue.
- ☐ I can list some effects of population growth.
- ☐ I understand the impacts of population growth on our environment.
- ☐ I know at least one way to minimize the effects of population growth on our environment.

Unit 7

Pollution

Environmental pollution is the introduction of harmful, unsafe or not suitable elements into the environment.

At the end of this unit, you will be able to ...

☐ understand the different types of environmental pollution.
☐ understand the connection between human activity and pollution.
☐ understand high-level vocabulary related to pollution.

Vocabulary Focus

A. *Match the words (1-12) with the correct definitions (a-l). The first one has been done for you!*

1. (k) audible
2. (　) contaminate
3. (　) crop
4. (　) disturb
5. (　) evidence
6. (　) flora and fauna
7. (　) fertilizer
8. (　) harmony
9. (　) lifestyle
10. (　) machinery
11. (　) nocturnal
12. (　) runoff

a. machine in general; parts of a machine
b. something that drains or flows off
c. a plant or food
d. the plants and animals living in an area
e. the facts that make you believe in something
f. active at night
g. to interrupt; to interfere with the normal arrangement
h. exist in peace/agreement; pleasant combination
i. to make something dirty; to add a dangerous substance
j. the way people live and work
k. **something that can be heard**
l. a substance added to soil to make plants grow better

B. *Complete the sentences with the words from MATCHING. You may need to change the word form.*

1. Mankind must find a way to live in _____ with the environment.
2. The shy student's voice is barely _____.
3. I am sorry to _____ you, but we need to talk now.
4. The gardener spread _____ on the field to help the plants grow.
5. An example of _____ is when rainwater flows across a field into a river.

Writing Sentences

Write two original sentences using words from MATCHING. You may need to change the word form.

1. _____

2. _____

Reading

Read this passage carefully and underline any unknown words.

When talking about pollution, the first thing many people think about is air pollution, but there are many other types of pollution. Environmental pollution includes not only the ones that directly affect our planet's resources like air, water, and land pollution, but also the ones that affect our **lifestyle**, like noise, visual, and light pollution.

Air pollution is caused by the emission of hazardous gases into our atmosphere by, for example, cars and factories. These gases cause changes in the climate, and the **flora and fauna** of our planet. The increasing number of people diagnosed with respiratory problems is seen to be a direct consequence of air pollution. Special interest groups often use this **evidence** to support their claims that pollution can affect humans directly.

Water pollution happens when industrial and household waste is released into rivers, lakes and any other kind of body of water. Also, **runoff** from the use of agricultural chemicals such as pesticides as well as acid rain can be one cause of water pollution because they harm the animals and plants living in the area.

Land pollution, or soil **contamination**, is the direct or indirect result of human activity destroying pieces of land that could be used constructively. Polluted water, **fertilizers**, and spilling of other chemicals can all lead to bad **crops** and soil infertility.

Noise, light, and visual pollution are all the direct result of our modern lives. Noise pollution is caused by aircraft, vehicle horns, and every type of modern **machinery** that makes **audible** and non-audible noise when in operation. Light pollution happens when too much light is used. It washes away our starlight and affects **nocturnal** animals and plants. Finally, visual pollution refers to everything that affects our ability to enjoy a landscape with **disturbing** visuals or negative changes to the environment like landfills, billboards, power lines, and street signs.

Pollution is directly related to the way we interact with the environment. Avoiding environmental pollution means to **harmoniously** interact with the plants, animals and everything else in our environment.

(337 words)

NOTES diagnosed「診断された」／ respiratory「呼吸器系の」／ interest group「利益団体」／ acid rain「酸性雨」／ billboard「広告掲示板」／ power line「送電線」

7 Pollution

Understanding

A. *Choose the best answer to each question.*

1. At least how many kinds of pollution affect our lifestyles?
   a. two
   b. three
   c. four

2. The number of people with respiratory problems is ...
   a. decreasing.
   b. increasing.
   c. remaining the same.

3. What does visual pollution do?
   a. causes changes to the climate
   b. destroys land
   c. reduces our enjoyment of the landscape

B. *Answer the following questions. Use complete and grammatically correct sentences.*

1. What is the main source of air pollution?

   _____
   _____

2. How can we avoid water pollution?

   _____
   _____

3. Explain a relationship between air, water, and land pollution.

   _____
   _____

C. *The following statements have mistakes. Correct them.*

1. Spilling of chemicals is the main cause of soil infertility.

   _____

2. Night pollution happens when cars run at night.

   _____

3. Mankind has no control over pollution.

   _____

D. *These words or phrases were used in the READING. Circle the word that has a similar meaning.*

1. There are many other <u>types</u> of pollution.
   a. species b. sections c. categories d. divisions
2. Air pollution is caused by the emission of <u>hazardous</u> gases into our atmosphere.
   a. hard b. transparent c. greenhouse d. dangerous
3. Water pollution happens when waste is <u>released into</u> rivers and lakes.
   a. put b. recycled c. found d. noticed
4. Noise pollution is caused by modern <u>machinery</u> that makes noise when in operation.
   a. organizations b. structures c. hardware d. sounds
5. To avoid environmental pollution is to <u>harmoniously</u> interact with the environment.
   a. hardly b. smoothly c. barely d. strictly

Listening

A. *Listen to each question and circle the letter of the best answer.* 🄲22

1. What kind of pollution do most people think of?
   a. air b. land c. water
2. a. decreased b. increased c. remained the same
3. a. light b. visual c. water

B. *Listen and write each sentence you hear.* 🄲23

1. The _____ near my house is _____ with pesticides.
2. The choir _____ to stay in _____ on the difficult song.
3. The _____ playing loud music _____ his _____.
4. _____
5. _____

Discussing

With a partner or in a small group, answer ONE of the following questions.

a. What are the main types of visual pollution?
b. What are the main types of noise pollution?
c. Which kind of environmental pollution affects you the most?

Take your notes in the space below:

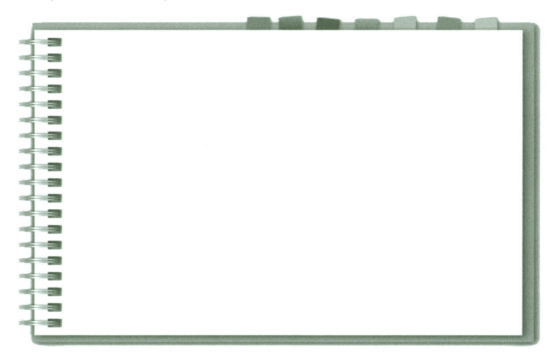

Reviewing

Before you move on to the next unit, make sure you can check all the boxes.

- ☐ I can explain why pollution is an environmental issue.
- ☐ I can list many types of environmental pollution.
- ☐ I understand the impacts of pollution on our environment.
- ☐ I know at least one way to minimize pollution effects on our environment.

Unit 8

Water

Less than 3% of all water in our planet is drinkable.
At the end of this unit, you will be able to ...

☐ understand how important water availability is.
☐ understand how water scarcity impacts our future.
☐ understand high-level vocabulary related to water scarcity.

Vocabulary Focus

A. *Match the words (1-12) with the correct definitions (a-l). The first one has been done for you!*

1. (h) available		7. ( ) proposal	
2. ( ) debris		8. ( ) scarce	
3. ( ) dump		9. ( ) soak	
4. ( ) irrigate		10. ( ) spark	
5. ( ) mankind		11. ( ) threaten	
6. ( ) priority		12. ( ) treatment	

▶ 48

a. process by which something is cleaned
b. a small flash of light produced by hitting two hard substances together
c. garbage; pieces of something after it has been destroyed
d. to become completely wet
e. to get rid of something
f. when you tell somebody that you will punish or harm them, especially if they do not do what you want
g. something that you think is more important than other things
h. something that is possible to get or find
i. there is not enough of it and it is only available in small quantities
j. all humans; the human race
k. a formal suggestion or plan
l. to supply water to an area of farmland through pipes or channels to grow crops

B. *Complete the sentences with the words from MATCHING. You may need to change the word form.*

1. Reducing the use of fossil fuels is a _____ in Japan.
2. Using too much water to _____ crops may pollute rivers.
3. Fertile soil for growing crops is becoming _____.
4. His _____ for a new railroad was received with skepticism.
5. You should _____ the beans in water overnight before cooking them.

Writing Sentences

Write two original sentences using words from MATCHING. You may need to change the word form.

1. _____

   _____

2. _____

   _____

Reading

Read this passage carefully and underline any unknown words.

Water availability has become a major problem in many places, including areas where water is highly **available** due to pollution, contamination or unsustainable use. As water is essential for many industrial and agricultural processes, water **scarcity** directly affects the development of communities and is a very important environmental issue. Water becomes an issue in two different areas: quality and quantity.

In 1969, the Cuyahoga River in Cleveland, USA, caught on fire after **sparks** coming from a train ignited the oil-**soaked debris** floating on the surface of the river. The incident showed how excessive industrial waste **dumping** can be and interest groups demanded better water pollution control. Even now, things such as agricultural runoff, mining and construction sites constantly **threaten** sources of clean water. That is why many governments around the world are trying to secure water supplies. Water quality is a **priority** for many countries, especially in developing ones where around 70 percent of industrial waste is dumped into rivers without any **treatment**.

With world population rising and economies growing, water availability is also a pressing issue not only in dry regions. As the worldwide population continues to increase, more food is necessary to support it, which means more water is used to **irrigate** crops. In fact, 70 percent of all water we consume is used primarily for agriculture and in many areas water consumption is greater than availability, which may lead to the depletion of underground water supplies.

A problem with water is that it is not only necessary for **mankind**, but also needed by nature to support plants and animals, that will, in turn, support us. To alleviate this problem, and to ensure a future with plenty of fresh water for everyone, some current **proposals** are: promoting water efficiency strategies, pushing governments and companies to control water pollution and water treatment before dumping it into rivers, and encouraging water reuse. *(312 words)*

NOTES Cuyahoga River (Cleveland)「カヤホガ川（クリーブランド）」

8 Water

Understanding

A. *Choose the best answer to each question.*

1. Water is an issue in how many areas?
    a. one
    b. two
    c. three

2. Where is water quality a priority?
    a. developed countries
    b. developing countries
    c. industrialized countries

3. How much water is used for farming?
    a. 30%
    b. 50%
    c. 70%

B. *Answer the following questions. Use complete and grammatically correct sentences.*

1. Summarize what happened in 1969.

2. Why is water an important environmental issue?

3. What are three ways to deal with water problems?

C. *The following statements have mistakes. Correct them.*

1. Water is an environmental issue in desert regions.

2. Governments around the world are securing water supplies so they can sell it later.

3. Using water for irrigation is an efficient way to use water because it is not wasted.

D. *These words or phrases were used in the READING. Circle the word that has a similar meaning.*

1. Water <u>scarcity</u> directly affects development of communities.
   a. treatment   b. quality   c. availability   d. depth

2. Many governments around the world are trying to <u>secure</u> water supplies.
   a. keep   b. sell   c. release   d. use

3. With world population rising, water availability is a <u>pressing</u> issue.
   a. famous   b. important   c. new   d. popular

4. High consumption may <u>deplete</u> of underground water.
   a. use a little   b. use a lot   c. use almost all   d. use all

5. To <u>ensure</u> a future with plenty of fresh water, we must control water pollution.
   a. make   b. check   c. create   d. guarantee

Listening

A. *Listen to each question and circle the letter of the best answer.* 25

1. Where is water availability an issue?
   a. anywhere   b. somewhere   c. everywhere

2. a. fires   b. mining   c. runoff

3. a. mankind supports nature   b. mankind supports people
   c. nature supports people

B. *Listen and write each sentence you hear.* 26

1. A series of _____ started a fire in the _____.

2. A _____ of processes _____ _____ by water scarcity.

3. In some _____, untreated waste is _____ _____ _____.

4. _____

5. _____

8 Water

Discussing

With a partner or in a small group, answer ONE of the following questions.

a. How much water do you drink each day?

b. Are you concerned about water availability?

c. What can we do in our daily lives to conserve water?

Take your notes in the space below:

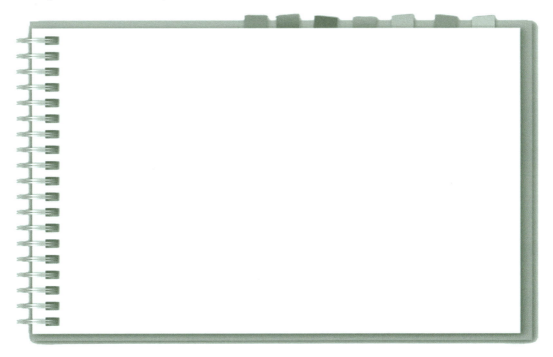

Reviewing

Before you move on to the next unit, make sure you can check all the boxes.

- ☐ I can explain why water scarcity is an environmental issue.
- ☐ I can list some causes of water scarcity.
- ☐ I understand the impacts of water scarcity for humans and nature.
- ☐ I know at least one way to minimize the effects of water scarcity.

▶ 53

Unit 9

Deforestation

Deforestation happens when all trees in an area are cut down or burnt.
At the end of this unit, you will be able to ...

- ☐ understand the importance of trees to the environment.
- ☐ understand the alternatives to deforestation.
- ☐ understand high-level vocabulary related to deforestation.

Vocabulary Focus

A. Match the words (1-12) with the correct definitions (a-l). The first one has been done for you!

1. (f)	adequate		7. ( )	isolated
2. ( )	dramatic		8. ( )	retain
3. ( )	drought		9. ( )	role
4. ( )	erosion		10. ( )	secure
5. ( )	extinct		11. ( )	shelter
6. ( )	extract		12. ( )	urbanization

a. a long period of time when there is little or no rain
b. having a place to live or stay, thought to be a basic human need
c. the process by which the surface of something is slowly destroyed by wind, rain, etc.
d. without much contact; far away
e. the function that someone or something has in an organization, in society, etc.
f. **something enough in quantity or good enough in quality**
g. get something from something else
h. the process in which towns, streets, factories, etc. are built, which was countryside before
i. to keep something
j. a type of plant, animal, etc. that is no longer in existence
k. to make certain of; ensure
l. a sudden change in something; change by surprise

B. *Complete the sentences with the words from MATCHING. You may need to change the word form.*

1. The dentist will probably _____ the dead tooth.
2. My grandparents live in a(n) _____ village in the countryside.
3. Forests play an important _____ in our environment.
4. Dinosaurs became _____ a long time ago.
5. Extreme temperatures caused a(n) _____ that lasted more than a month.

Writing Sentences

Write two original sentences using words from MATCHING. You may need to change the word form.

1. _____
   _____
2. _____
   _____

Reading

Read this passage carefully and underline any unknown words.

Deforestation is an environmental issue that happens all over the world. It is the destruction of forests in order to make the land available for other uses or simply to **extract** timber. Agriculture and **urbanization** play an important **role** in deforestation as most of land clearing occurs because of them.

Cutting down forests has many negative effects on the environment. The most **dramatic** impact is the loss of habitat for millions of species. Seventy percent of Earth's land animals and plants live in forests. With the loss of habitat, many species end up **isolated** without enough food and **shelter** to sustain their existence and many become **extinct**.

Another side effect of deforestation is climate change. Many environmentalists believe that deforestation is also directly connected to global warming. One technique used to clear a forested area is called "slash and burn", where the trees and plants are cut down and burned. In addition, with the reduction of forests, not only is the amount of CO_2 removed from the atmosphere reduced, but also the CO_2 **retained** by the trees is released into the atmosphere. In fact, the process of deforestation releases as much CO_2 into our atmosphere as all the cars, trucks, and buses on our planet.

More than serving as home to animal life and cleaning our air, forests are essential to **secure** a stable and **adequate** food supply for our growing population, protect the soil against **erosion** and **drought**, and allow for sustainable agriculture.

One of the proposed solutions to deforestation is reforestation. Still, only planting trees is not enough to rebuild a forest. As with many other environmental issues, a huge effort is necessary to alleviate the damage that has already been done by deforestation all over the world.

(290 words)

NOTES slash and burn「焼畑」

Understanding

A. *Choose the best answer to each question.*

1. What percentage of the world's animals and plants live in forests?
   a. 60%
   b. 70%
   c. 80%

2. What does "slash and burn" mean?
   a. cutting down trees and burning them
   b. reducing CO_2 from the atmosphere
   c. releasing CO_2 into the atmosphere

3. What is reforestation?
   a. allowing for agriculture
   b. planting trees to regrow a forest
   c. securing a stable food supply

B. *Answer the following questions. Use complete and grammatically correct sentences.*

1. What happens to animals who are living in a forest when deforestation happens?

   _____

   _____

2. How is the practice of "slash and burn" connected to global warming?

   _____

   _____

3. Is reforestation a viable solution to deforestation? Why?

   _____

   _____

C. *The following statements have mistakes. Correct them.*

1. Deforestation is one of the solutions to population growth.

   _____

2. Through "slash and burn", no CO_2 is released into the atmosphere.

   _____

3. Cars, trucks, and buses release substantially more CO_2 than deforestation.

   _____

D. *These words or phrases were used in the READING. Circle the word that has a similar meaning.*

1. Forests are destroyed to extract timber.

    a. shoes b. wood c. fire d. land

2. One technique used to clear an area with a forest is called "slash and burn".

    a. machine b. tree c. wood d. way of doing

3. Seventy percent of Earth's land animals and plants live in forests.

    a. our planet b. our forest c. our river d. our ocean

4. Forests also allow for sustainable agriculture.

    a. keeps itself b. destroys itself c. finds itself d. hurts itself

5. With the loss of habitat, many species end up isolated without enough food.

    a. common place b. place with many trees c. place of living d. location

Listening

A. *Listen to each question and circle the letter of the best answer.* 28

1. Where is deforestation taking place?

    a. anywhere b. somewhere c. everywhere

2. a. species become isolated b. species have more shelter
    c. species have enough food

3. a. direct b. indirect c. parallel

B. *Listen and write each sentence you hear.* 29

1. The area _____ by rain forests is _____ decreasing.

2. Many students _____ the same _____ in the school play.

3. It _____ about 5 hours to drive to the _____ community in the _____.

4. _____

5. _____

Discussing

With a partner or in a small group, answer ONE of the following questions.

a. Would you rather live in the countryside or in a city?

b. Have you ever played in a forest? What did you do?

c. What wild animals have you seen near your home?

Take your notes in the space below:

Reviewing

Before you move on to the next unit, make sure you can check all the boxes.

- ☐ I can explain why deforestation is an environmental issue.
- ☐ I can list some causes of deforestation.
- ☐ I understand the impacts of deforestation on our environment.
- ☐ I know at least one way to avoid/minimize deforestation effects on our environment.

Unit 10

Review 2: Units 6–9

Part 1: Photographs

You will hear four short statements. Look at the picture and choose the statement that best describes what you see in the picture.

1.

(A)   (B)   (C)   (D)

3.

(A)   (B)   (C)   (D)

2.

(A)   (B)   (C)   (D)

4.

(A)   (B)   (C)   (D)

Part 2: Question-Response

You will hear a question or statement followed by three responses. Choose the best response.

1. (A)   (B)   (C)
2. (A)   (B)   (C)
3. (A)   (B)   (C)

4. (A)   (B)   (C)
5. (A)   (B)   (C)
6. (A)   (B)   (C)

10 Review 2: Units 6–9

Part 3: Conversations

You will hear short conversations. Questions 1-3 refer to the first conversation and Questions 4-6 refer to the second conversation. Choose the best answer to each of the three questions.

1. What are they talking about?
   (A) Children
   (B) Filtration system
   (C) Fish
   (D) Water

2. Where did the man likely buy it?
   (A) Clothing store
   (B) Furniture store
   (C) Pet shop
   (D) Supermarket

3. How does the man feel about his purchase?
   (A) Angry
   (B) Annoyed
   (C) Contented
   (D) Delighted

4. What are the two people talking about?
   (A) About a landslide
   (B) About a reporter
   (C) About the weather
   (D) About work

5. What is happening to the people living in the condominium?
   (A) They are in the rain.
   (B) They are in shock.
   (C) They had to leave the place.
   (D) They slashed and burned the area.

6. What is the most probable cause of the accident?
   (A) A landslide
   (B) Fire in the area
   (C) Soil erosion
   (D) There are a lot of trees.

Part 4: Talks

You will hear a short report. Choose the best answer to each of the three questions.

1. Who is likely the speaker?
   (A) A comedian
   (B) A lawyer
   (C) A lecturer
   (D) A radio DJ

2. What is urbanization?
   (A) People moving away from the cities
   (B) People moving to the countryside
   (C) People relocating to cities
   (D) People relocating to the countryside

3. What is likely to happen in the future?
   (A) 34% of the population will live in rural areas.
   (B) 34% of the population will live in urban areas.
   (C) 70% of the population will live in rural areas.
   (D) 70% of the population will live in urban areas.

Part 5: Incomplete Sentences

A word is missing in each of the sentences below. Choose the best answer to complete each sentence.

1. Many ------- have been suggested to manage population growth.
    (A) problems
    (B) questions
    (C) reports
    (D) solutions

2. Air pollution is caused by the ------- of hazardous gases.
    (A) concealment
    (B) elimination
    (C) emission
    (D) illumination

3. Water availability is a(n) ------- issue in many dry regions.
    (A) cautious
    (B) impressive
    (C) pressing
    (D) trivial

4. One of the ------- solutions to deforestation is reforestation.
    (A) proposal
    (B) proposed
    (C) proposing
    (D) proposition

5. Street signs can also be considered visual pollution because they ------- our ability to enjoy the environment.
    (A) affect
    (B) defect
    (C) effect
    (D) improve

Part 6: Text Completion

Four words are missing in the text. Choose the best answers to complete the text.

Nowadays, plastic has become an environmental issue, mainly because most of it ends in the oceans. There are several areas around our planet that, due to ocean currents, accumulate plastic debris (trash) and are called patches. The biggest of these patches is The Great Pacific Garbage Patch (GPGP) which is in the middle of the Pacific Ocean, about halfway between Hawaii and California. Marine scientists cannot agree on the actual size of the GPGP. The main reason for this is because researchers use different numbers (number of microscopic plastic particles per cubic meter) when determining the boundaries of the area. Despite being large in size, it cannot be seen by satellite or boats passing because the ------- 1. of these particles are just under the surface of water.

Why is this debris an issue that needs to be dealt with? This debris creates three main problems. The first problem is that some animals (sea turtles and albatrosses) ------- plastic debris to their young. In addition, these particles also
                      2.
------- our food chain. For example, small fish are eaten by larger fish who are then
3.
eaten by humans. Finally, the floating plastic debris can also enable the ------- of
                                                                        4.
invasive species.

1. (A) big
   (B) none
   (C) majority
   (D) whole

2. (A) eat
   (B) feed
   (C) increase
   (D) seed

3. (A) change
   (B) eat
   (C) enter
   (D) make

4. (A) clear
   (B) control
   (C) hold
   (D) spread

Part 7: Reading Comprehension

Read the advertisement. Choose the best answer to each question.

Every day, a healthy day

Plant a Tree Campaign

Fresh Bread House is inviting all of its customers to join us this weekend. Over 200 trees will be planted this weekend in Central Park (in front of City Hall). Come with family and friends and join us in making Anderson County a greener and better place for future generations.

IMPORTANT INFORMATION

Place: Anderson County's Central Park

Schedule:
8 AM - Registration opens
9 AM - Shovels & trees will be distributed
10 AM - Work starts
12 PM - Clean up

**No experience necessary
No age limits
Free drinks and bread**

All trees will be distributed upon registration. Planting locations will be marked with ribbons (Make sure to check the Central Park map to find them). Each kind of tree should be matched with its ribbon color.

Our staff will be distributing Fresh Bread House T-shirts. Make sure to get one!

For inquiries, please contact us at 903-268-TREE (8733).

10 Review 2: Units 6–9

1. Where is the pamphlet likely to be distributed?
   (A) At schools
   (B) At traffic lights
   (C) To customers of a store
   (D) To friends and family

2. Which of the following is true?
   (A) People need experience to participate.
   (B) People need to bring shovels.
   (C) People should come alone.
   (D) People should wake up early to participate.

3. How do people know where to plant the trees?
   (A) A Central Park employee will show them.
   (B) A staff member will be helping.
   (C) All locations have ribbons which should match the color of the tree.
   (D) All trees have ribbons with matching colors.

4. Where is this campaign taking place?
   (A) At Fresh Bread House
   (B) At the City Hall
   (C) In a park
   (D) In the woods

Unit 11
Hydroelectricity

Hydroelectric power plants generate electricity using the flow of water (hydro).
At the end of this unit, you will be able to ...

☐ understand how hydroelectric power plants work.
☐ understand some limitations of hydroelectric energy.
☐ understand high-level vocabulary related to hydroelectric energy.

Vocabulary Focus

A. *Match the words (1-12) with the correct definitions (a-l). The first one has been done for you!*

1. (f)	**convert**		7. ( )	reservoir
2. ( )	drawback		8. ( )	riverbed
3. ( )	elevation		9. ( )	rot
4. ( )	flexibility		10. ( )	spawn
5. ( )	methane		11. ( )	stability
6. ( )	reliability		12. ( )	turbine

a. a piece of ground that is higher than the area around it
b. a man-made lake where water is stored for later use
c. a gas with no color or smell that is used for fuel
d. to decay (break down) naturally and slowly
e. to lay eggs (fish, frogs, etc.)
f. **to change from one form, purpose, system etc. to another**
g. the state of being steady and not changing
h. a device that receives its power from a wheel that is turned by the flow of water, air or gas
i. able to change to match new conditions or situations
j. the area over which a river usually flows
k. a disadvantage or problem
l. able to work or operate for long periods without breaking

B. Complete the sentences with the words from MATCHING. You may need to change the word form.

1. One _____ of the system is the high cost.
2. The new politician promises to bring _____ to the country.
3. A large change in _____ can give some people headaches.
4. If you don't clean your refrigerator soon, all the vegetables will _____.
5. Many tourists come to see the fish _____ in the autumn.

Writing Sentences

Write two original sentences using words from MATCHING. You may need to change the word form.

1. _____

_____

2. _____

_____

Reading

Read this passage carefully and underline any unknown words.

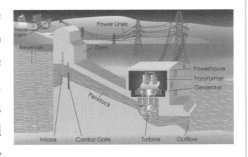

Hydroelectricity is electricity generated by the flow of water. Usually, in an area with steep land **elevation** changes, a dam is built to create a **reservoir** of water. Gates are used to control how much water flows from the reservoir. This water is used to move **turbines** connected to machinery that generates electricity. The amount of electricity generated depends on how much water flows through the dam. Some hydroelectric power plants are built on natural waterfalls, so they use natural water flow to generate electricity without the necessity of building a dam.

Some practical advantages of hydroelectricity are **reliability**, **flexibility**, and price **stability**. It is reliable because it relies very little on natural resources. It is flexible because it can be adjusted to demand, by opening the gates more when consumers need more electricity or by partially closing them when consumption is low (for example at night). The price is stable because water is a domestic resource that does not need to be imported. Additionally, it is also environmentally friendly because it produces much fewer greenhouse gases than coal, gas or oil power plants. It is also a renewable resource, as it uses running water to produce energy without depleting it.

Modern turbines can **convert** as much as 90% of available energy into electricity compared with a 50% conversion rate from fossil fuel power plants. Worldwide, hydroelectricity accounts for 97% of all electricity generated by renewable sources.

Although hydroelectricity's advantages make it look like a promising and green way to generate electricity, it has some **drawbacks**. The generation of electricity does not produce greenhouse gases, but the **rotting** of plants in the reservoir can produce **methane**: a greenhouse gas. In addition, when a reservoir is built, it is likely that the habitat of plants and animals in the area will be destroyed, and people may need to relocate. Another problem is that fish may no longer be able to migrate downstream to the ocean, or upstream to **spawn**. Habitats downstream from the dam are also affected as low oxygen levels can cause harm to plant and animal life. When the dam is closed, **riverbed** erosion can also destroy habitats, and lower the groundwater table.

(364 words)

11 Hydroelectricity

Understanding

A. *Choose the best answer to each question.*

1. Why is a dam built?
   a. to connect machinery
   b. to make a reservoir
   c. to move turbines

2. Compared to fossil fuel power plants, modern turbines are ...
   a. 10% more efficient.
   b. 40% more efficient.
   c. 97% more efficient.

3. What is one of the drawbacks mentioned in the passage?
   a. It can destroy the local habitat.
   b. It can generate too much electricity.
   c. It can increase oxygen levels.

B. *Answer the following questions. Use complete and grammatically correct sentences.*

1. How is hydroelectricity generated?

2. Why are reservoirs at high altitudes preferred for hydroelectric power plants?

3. Explain how hydroelectric power plants can provide more electricity when needed.

C. *The following statements have mistakes. Correct them.*

1. Hydroelectric power plants account for 97% of all power plants worldwide.

2. People sometimes need to relocate because of methane gas.

3. Hydroelectricity is a 90% renewable energy solution.

D. *These words or phrases were used in the READING. Circle the word that has a similar meaning.*

1. Hydroelectricity is electricity <u>generated</u> by the flow of water.
   a. delivered   b. made   c. played   d. used

2. The amount of electricity generated depends on how much water <u>flows</u> through the dam.
   a. looks   b. passes   c. results   d. tears

3. It is flexible because it can be <u>adjusted</u> to demand.
   a. changed   b. made   c. passed   d. used

4. Hydroelectricity's <u>advantages</u> make it look like a promising and green way to generate electricity.
   a. benefits   b. bonuses   c. factors   d. solutions

5. Fish may no longer be able to <u>migrate</u> downstream to the ocean.
   a. account for   b. locate   c. return   d. travel

Listening

A. *Listen to each question and circle the letter of the best answer.* 🔊 35

1. Where are dams for hydroelectricity usually built?
   a. flat areas   b. rocky areas   c. steep areas

2. a. mornings   b. evenings   c. at night

3. a. fish can migrate   b. groundwater table is lowered
   c. oxygen levels increase

B. *Listen and write each sentence you hear.* 🔊 36

1. The advantages _____ the _____ .

2. Many _____ marathon runners _____ at higher _____ .

3. The _____ worked _____ repairing the _____ _____ .

4. _____

5. _____

Discussing

With a partner or in a small group, answer ONE of the following questions.

a. Many people enjoy visiting dams, how about you?

b. Have you ever visited a dam?

c. What do you think is the biggest disadvantage of dams?

Take your notes in the space below:

Reviewing

Before you move on to the next unit, make sure you can check all the boxes.

☐ I can explain how energy is produced from the flow of water.
☐ I can list some problems with hydroelectric power plants.
☐ I understand the impacts of hydroelectricity on our environment.
☐ I can explain how hydroelectricity can be flexible.

Unit 12

Solar Panels

Solar panels absorb sunlight and transform it into electricity.
At the end of this unit, you will be able to ...

☐ understand how solar panels work.
☐ understand limitations of solar energy.
☐ understand high-level vocabulary related to solar energy.

Vocabulary Focus

A. Match the words (1-12) with the correct definitions (a-l). The first one has been done for you!

1. (l) assemble
2. (   ) discourage
3. (   ) financial
4. (   ) generate
5. (   ) investment
6. (   ) lifespan
7. (   ) photovoltaic
8. (   ) practice
9. (   ) prominent
10. (   ) pursue
11. (   ) scale
12. (   ) technology

▶ 72

a. an activity related to money
b. the money, effort or support put into something expecting a future benefit
c. the methods and tools used to solve a problem
d. to try to prevent; to show disagreement
e. something important that most people know about
f. to try to do something difficult over time
g. to do something many times
h. the size of something when compared to something else
i. to produce or create something
j. the length of time something is likely to function
k. produces energy when exposed to light
l. to put together parts of something

B. Complete the sentences with the words from MATCHING. You may need to change the word form.

1. It is his _____ to read a book every week.
2. Some people have difficulty _____ furniture.
3. Never take _____ advice from someone who is poor.
4. Our government is _____ a lot of money in photovoltaic research.
5. Her parents strongly _____ her from buying a brand-new car.

Writing Sentences

Write two original sentences using words from MATCHING. You may need to change the word form.

1. _____
   _____

2. _____
   _____

Reading

Read this passage carefully and underline any unknown words.

Photovoltaic cells, also known as solar cells, are devices which collect energy from sunlight and transform it into electricity. These cells are **assembled** into panels, which can be set on rooftops, to provide electricity on a small **scale**, or in large areas called solar farms. **Generating** electricity from sunlight is a very interesting idea because every minute the sun showers our planet with enough energy to supply humankind's demand for an entire year.

Although a **prominent** renewable source of energy, solar power is not truly green. The industrial processes used when manufacturing solar panels not only use toxic materials, but also release gases more dangerous than CO_2. Also, at the current state of **technology**, the **lifespan** of solar panels is around twenty years, which makes the use of them a large **investment** for most households. Once a panel reaches the end of its lifespan, careful disposal and recycling procedures are necessary to ensure that the environment is not polluted.

The solar energy industry, along with governments, should work on **practices** that oversee the entire lifecycle of solar panels. It is important to reduce and eventually eliminate the use of toxic materials during manufacturing. Also, they need to develop and maintain recycling technologies and practices.

The manufacturing problems and short lifespan of solar panels might **discourage** some people, but as technology progresses, operation costs, maintenance, and disposal are likely to become more affordable. In addition, as the technology is quite new, with continued research, the lifespan and **financial** benefits of solar panels are expected to increase. Investing in solar panels for your house now might not bring direct financial benefits for you, but it helps in the bigger fight of **pursuing** a renewable source of energy that will restore our planet's equilibrium and maintain the environment for future generations.

(*298 words*)

NOTES Photovoltaic cell「光起電力セル」／ solar farm「ソーラーファーム（大規模発電所）」

12 Solar Panels

Understanding

A. *Choose the best answer to each question.*

1. What are photovoltaic cells also known as?
   a. batteries
   b. generators
   c. solar cells

2. How long is a solar panel expected to last?
   a. around 10 years
   b. around 20 years
   c. around 30 years

3. What will make solar panels more affordable?
   a. careful disposal procedures
   b. improved technology
   c. increased operational costs

B. *Answer the following questions. Use complete and grammatically correct sentences.*

1. How is electricity harvested from sunlight?

   _____

   _____

2. What happens when a panel reaches the end of its lifespan?

   _____

   _____

3. Nowadays, what is the main benefit of solar panels?

   _____

   _____

C. *The following statements have mistakes. Correct them.*

1. The process of making a solar panel releases a lot of CO_2 into the atmosphere.

   _____

2. Investing in solar panels saves a lot of money for households.

   _____

3. Governments oversee the entire solar panel recycling process.

   _____

D. *These words or phrases were used in the READING. Circle the word that has a similar meaning.*

1. <u>Photo</u>voltaic cells are also known as solar cells.
   a. light   b. energy   c. electricity   d. lamp

2. The solar energy industry should work on <u>practices</u> that oversee the entire lifecycle of solar panels.
   a. efficiency   b. costs   c. governments   d. way of doing

3. Photovoltaic cells are <u>assembled</u> into panels.
   a. burned   b. put together   c. made   d. taken apart

4. It is important to <u>reduce</u> the use of toxic materials.
   a. set to zero   b. maximize   c. minimize   d. keep it the same

5. Although a <u>prominent</u> renewable source of energy, solar power is not truly green.
   a. good   b. common   c. obvious   d. important

Listening

A. *Listen to each question and circle the letter of the best answer.* 🔘 38

1. What is a large group of solar panels called?
   a. solar cell   b. solar factory   c. solar farm

2. a. uses toxic materials   b. releases CO_2 c. high operational costs

3. a. saves money   b. helps with research   c. lowers costs

B. *Listen and write each sentence you hear.* 🔘 39

1. Some species of turtles have _____ of more than _____ _____.

2. Generating _____ from _____ is a very _____ idea.

3. Some people have _____ _____ _____.

4. _____

5. _____

Discussing

With a partner or in a small group, answer ONE of the following questions.

a. Do you know anyone who is using solar panels?
b. Why don't many people invest in solar panels?
c. Would you install solar panels on your house?

Take your notes in the space below:

Reviewing

Before you move on to the next unit, make sure you can check all the boxes.

☐ I can explain how energy is harvested from the sun.
☐ I can list some problems with solar panels.
☐ I understand the impacts of solar panels on our environment.
☐ I can explain at least one way solar energy helps protect our environment.

Unit 13

Wind Turbines

Wind turbines make electricity from the wind.
At the end of this unit, you will be able to ...

☐ understand the basic features of wind turbines.
☐ understand different types of wind turbines.
☐ understand advanced vocabulary related to wind turbines.

Vocabulary Focus

A. Match the words (1-12) with the correct definitions (a-l). The first one has been done for you!

1. (f) blade
2. (   ) constant
3. (   ) evolve
4. (   ) generator
5. (   ) grain
6. (   ) grind
7. (   ) horizontal
8. (   ) maintenance
9. (   ) scholar
10. (   ) shaft
11. (   ) unreliable
12. (   ) vertical

a. the act of keeping a machine or building in good condition
b. someone who knows a lot about a subject
c. the seeds of plants used for food
d. positioned up and down
e. to change or develop slowly
f. a spinning part on a machine used to push air or water
g. a bar in machine that holds parts that move or spin
h. not to be depended on
i. positioned from side to side
j. something that stays the same
k. to crush or break into very small pieces
l. machine that makes electricity

B. *Complete the sentences with the words from MATCHING. You may need to change the word form.*

1. The old car was _____ and needed to be repaired.
2. The temperature stayed _____ during the process.
3. Some people like to _____ their coffee beans.
4. The _____ of the electric fan were made of metal.
5. In a spreadsheet, the rows are _____.

Writing Sentences

Write two original sentences using words from MATCHING. You may need to change the word form.

1. _____

_____

2. _____

_____

Reading

Read this passage carefully and underline any unknown words.

You may think that using the wind to create power is a recent development. Of course, the technology being used is **constantly evolving**, but the basic principles have not changed. Windmills have been used for a long time. **Scholars** think that the first windmills were used in either Babylon (2000 B.C.) or Persia (200 B.C.) to **grind grain**. Much later, in the 11th century, windmills were introduced to Europe.

A basic wind turbine has three main parts: rotor **blades**, a **shaft**, and a **generator**. Basically, the wind turns the blades which spins the shaft. The shaft is connected to a generator which creates electricity.

There are two main types of modern wind turbines. The most common type of wind turbine is the **horizontal**-axis type. Most horizontal-axis wind turbines have two or three blades. These turbines face the wind to create energy. Often many of these turbines are placed close together to make a wind farm.

The second type of turbine is the **vertical**-axis type. They are often called Darrieus wind turbines after Georges Jean Marie Darrieus, the man who made the design. One advantage of vertical-axis turbines is that they do not need to face the wind. Unfortunately, these turbines require a lot of **maintenance**.

Because many countries are trying to reduce their dependence on fossil fuels, wind energy is one of the fastest growing energy sources in the world. The main advantage of wind energy is that it is a clean, renewable source of energy.

Unfortunately, there are also some problems with wind turbines. The energy supply can be **unreliable** because turbines cannot generate energy when there is no wind. Also, the blades can be a threat to wildlife such as birds. Finally, some people complain about the noise and visual pollution. *(293 words)*

NOTES: Babylon「バビロン（メソポタミア地方の古代都市）」／ Persia「ペルシャ（現在のイラン）」／ Darrieus wind turbine「ダリウス風車」／ Georges Jean Marie Darrieus「ジョージズ・ジーン・マリエ・ダリウス」

13 Wind Turbines

Understanding

A. *Choose the best answer to each question.*

1. Where were the first windmills used?
   a. in Europe
   b. in the Middle East
   c. in the United States of America

2. What is a wind farm?
   a. a place with one wind turbine
   b. a place with some wind turbines
   c. a place with a lot of wind turbines

3. What is an advantage of a vertical-axis wind turbine?
   a. It can be placed in any direction.
   b. It does not make any noise.
   c. It is easy to maintain.

B. *Answer the following questions. Use complete and grammatically correct sentences.*

1. What are the two main types of wind turbines?

2. Which type of wind turbine is more popular? Why?

3. What are some problems with wind turbines?

C. *The following statements have mistakes. Correct them.*

1. Windmills are a modern invention.

2. Georges Jean Marie Darrieus invented the horizontal-axis wind turbine.

3. Wind turbines prevent noise and visual pollution.

D. *These words or phrases were used in the READING. Circle the word that has a similar meaning.*

1. The <u>principle</u> to create power from wind has not changed.
    a. rule   b. restriction   c. idea   d. teacher
2. Windmills were <u>introduced</u> to Europe in the 11th century.
    a. found   b. begun   c. destroyed   d. studied
3. Wind turbines face the wind to <u>create</u> energy.
    a. use   b. refuse   c. generate   d. prevent
4. Many countries are trying to reduce their <u>dependence</u> on fossil fuels.
    a. reliance   b. description   c. complaint   d. guidance
5. Wind turbines <u>require</u> a lot of maintenance.
    a. dislike   b. give   c. stop   d. need

Listening

A. *Listen to each question and circle the letter of the best answer.* 41

1. When do some scholars think that the first windmills were made?
    a. 2000 B.C.   b. 200 A.D.   c. 1000 A.D.
2. a. blades   b. generator   c. turbine
3. a. they are easy to replace
    b. they do not need to face the wind
    c. they have low maintenance costs

B. *Listen and write each sentence you hear.* 42

1. _____ is a _____ kind of _____.
2. The young _____ knew _____ about the _____.
3. The old _____ _____ needs _____ _____ of _____.
4. _____
5. _____

Discussing

With a partner or in a small group, answer ONE of the following questions.

a. Have you ever seen a wind farm on television or in real life?
b. Some people think that wind turbines are beautiful, what do you think?
c. Do you think your house or school would be able to run using only wind energy?

Take your notes in the space below:

Reviewing

Before you move on to the next unit, make sure you can check all the boxes.

- ☐ I can describe the basic parts of a wind turbine.
- ☐ I know the two types of wind turbines.
- ☐ I understand the advantages of wind energy.
- ☐ I know some of the problems with wind turbines.

Unit 14

Nuclear Energy

Nuclear energy is a promising technology that produces little CO_2.
At the end of this unit, you will be able to ...

☐ understand some advantages of nuclear energy.
☐ understand some of the problems with nuclear energy.
☐ evaluate the risks posed by nuclear energy.

Vocabulary Focus

A. Match the words (1-12) with the correct definitions (a-l). The first one has been done for you!

1. (j) abundance
2. (   ) aging
3. (   ) associated
4. (   ) bury
5. (   ) demand
6. (   ) disaster
7. (   ) hazard
8. (   ) highly
9. (   ) nowadays
10. (   ) reactor
11. (   ) relatively
12. (   ) roughly

a. a request for something
b. comparing something to another thing
c. possible danger
d. more or less, about, not exactly
e. when something appears to get old
f. a lot, to a higher degree
g. a place where nuclear reactions happen in order to produce energy
h. when something is connected to another thing
i. right now, at this present time
j. a lot, in big quantity
k. an accident, an event of fact that causes a lot of trouble
l. to put something below the ground

B. *Complete the sentences with the words from MATCHING. You may need to change the word form.*

1. Safety is something _____ desired in a power plant.
2. Nuclear power is a _____ clean energy source.
3. A power plant _____ is where energy is created.
4. A city's _____ for electricity depends on the number of people living in it.
5. Low power production is often _____ with blackouts.

Writing Sentences

Write two original sentences using words from MATCHING. You may need to change the word form.

1. _____

2. _____

Reading

Read this passage carefully and underline any unknown words.

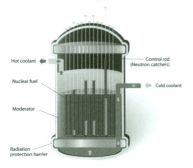

Although the first nuclear **reactor** was built in 1942, the first full-scale nuclear power plant began operations in England in 1956. Since then, many more nuclear power plants have been built around the world. As of 2016, there were 450 nuclear power plants in 31 countries.

Nowadays, the **demand** for energy keeps increasing, while at the same time public opinion pushes governments and companies to reduce carbon emissions. Nuclear energy seems to be the perfect solution because it is a **relatively** clean source of energy that requires little resources to operate, produces energy in **abundance**, and emits low quantities of CO_2. However, it has disadvantages that have negative impacts on our environment.

Two problems **associated** with nuclear energy are the lifespan of nuclear reactors and the disposal of radioactive waste. The reactors used by nuclear power plants have a lifespan of **roughly** 40 to 50 years and need to be replaced so the power plant can continue producing energy. Also, the fuel used by the reactors is **highly** radioactive and needs proper disposal. Currently there are two main ways to deal with radioactive waste: reprocess it to extract fuel or **bury** it deep in the ground and risk soil and groundwater contamination.

Additionally, there are safety **hazards** associated with nuclear energy. In 1986 there was a nuclear **disaster** in Chernobyl, Ukraine, when one of the reactors exploded. Many people died and the area close to the power plant is still very dangerous to humans due to the high levels of radiation. In 2011, another disaster happened in Fukushima, Japan, after a powerful earthquake and a tsunami damaged the cooling system of the reactors, resulting in explosions and a lot of radiation released into the atmosphere and the area.

Right now it is clear that a decision must be made. Should we replace **aging** reactors and keep investing in nuclear energy? Or should we start investing in developing new sources of energy?

(321 words)

NOTES: radioactive waste「放射性廃棄物」／ reprocess「再処理する」／ Chernobyl (Ukraine)「チェルノブイリ（ウクライナ）」

14 Nuclear Energy

Understanding

A. *Choose the best answer to each question.*

1. The first nuclear power plant was built in ...
    a. 1942.
    b. 1956.
    c. 2016.

2. Nuclear power plants ...
    a. emit CO_2 in abundance but also produces a lot of energy.
    b. have advantages and disadvantages.
    c. need few resources and produce little quantities of energy.

3. When we reprocess radioactive waste from nuclear power plants ...
    a. less CO_2 is released into the atmosphere.
    b. some fuel can be extracted and later reused.
    c. we put it down below the ground.

B. *Answer the following questions. Use complete and grammatically correct sentences.*

1. List some advantages of nuclear power plants.

2. List some disadvantages of nuclear power plants.

3. Why is using landfills for disposing radioactive waste a bad idea?

C. *The following statements have mistakes. Correct them.*

1. "Nuclear energy" is 100% clean energy.

2. Nuclear power plants produce a lot of energy but also need a lot of resources.

3. It is completely safe to bury used nuclear power plant fuel.

D. *These words or phrases were used in the READING. Circle the word that has a similar meaning.*

1. Nuclear energy seems to be the perfect solution as a <u>relatively</u> clean source of energy.
   a. to some extent   b. a lot   c. not so much   d. too much

2. The reactors used by nuclear power plants have a lifespan of <u>roughly</u> 40 to 50 years.
   a. unevenly   b. violently   c. approximately   d. dangerously

3. The fuel used by the reactors is <u>highly</u> radioactive.
   a. a little   b. not so much   c. not enough   d. a lot

4. Should we <u>invest in</u> developing new sources of energy?
   a. lose money on   b. put money into   c. save money for   d. find money for

5. One of the problems <u>associated</u> with nuclear energy is the lifespan of nuclear reactors.
   a. understood   b. developed   c. related   d. started

Listening

A. *Listen to each question and circle the letter of the best answer.*

1. If a nuclear reactor explodes, what may happen?
   a. a power blackout
   b. contamination of the area around
   c. It releases a lot of CO_2.

2. a. it is a relatively clean source of energy
   b. produces energy in abundance
   c. emits low quantities of CO_2

3. a. lifespan of nuclear reactors
   b. disposal of radioactive waste
   c. too many resources to operate

B. *Listen and write each sentence you hear.*

1. In 2016 there were _____ _____ _____ _____ around the world.

2. Chernobyl and Fukushima were _____ _____ _____ _____.

3. Nuclear power plants have _____ _____ _____ _____.

4. _____

5. _____

Discussing

With a partner or in a small group, answer ONE of the following questions.

a. Are nuclear power plants safe?

b. What is the best way to dispose of nuclear waste?

c. Should we repair aging reactors or should we invest in other energy sources?

Take your notes in the space below:

Reviewing

Before you move on to the next unit, make sure you can check all the boxes.

☐ I can explain some advantages of nuclear energy.
☐ I can explain some problems with nuclear energy.
☐ I understand the impacts of nuclear energy on our environment.
☐ I understand why some people say nuclear energy is not green.

Unit 15

Review 3: Units 11–14

Part 1: Photographs

You will hear four short statements. Look at the picture and choose the statement that best describes what you see in the picture.

1.

(A) (B) (C) (D)

2.

(A) (B) (C) (D)

3.

(A) (B) (C) (D)

4.

(A) (B) (C) (D)

Part 2: Question-Response

You will hear a question or statement followed by three responses. Choose the best response.

1. (A) (B) (C)
2. (A) (B) (C)
3. (A) (B) (C)

4. (A) (B) (C)
5. (A) (B) (C)
6. (A) (B) (C)

Part 3: Conversations

You will hear short conversations. Questions 1-3 refer to the first conversation and Questions 4-6 refer to the second conversation. Choose the best answer to each of the three questions.

1. Who most likely are the speakers?
   (A) Colleagues
   (B) Manager and employee
   (C) Salesperson and customer
   (D) Family members

2. What are the two people talking about?
   (A) Getting some batteries
   (B) Getting ready for camping
   (C) Getting ready for emergencies
   (D) Having lunch together

3. What is the woman likely to do next?
   (A) Buy some lunch
   (B) Buy some water
   (C) Buy some canned food
   (D) Buy a solar panel

4. What are the people likely doing?
   (A) Buying something
   (B) Following some instructions
   (C) Putting together something
   (D) Reading some instructions

5. Why is the woman annoyed?
   (A) The instructions are confusing.
   (B) The instructions are incorrect.
   (C) The instructions are too easy.
   (D) The piece should go horizontally.

6. What are the people likely to do next?
   (A) Call a friend
   (B) Call a handyman
   (C) Call a professor
   (D) Read the instructions

Part 4: Talks

You will hear a short speech. Choose the best answer to each of the three questions.

1. Who is making the announcement?
   (A) A company employee
   (B) A department manager
   (C) A reporter
   (D) An investor

2. Why is the announcement being made?
   (A) Because employees are supposed to work on Saturdays
   (B) Because some people might be annoyed by the noise
   (C) Because the company is using too much electricity
   (D) Because the deadline or report submission is next Saturday

3. What will the company do next week?
   (A) Delay the upcoming deadline
   (B) Have a department meeting
   (C) Install solar panels
   (D) Invest in the solar energy market

Part 5: Incomplete Sentences

A word is missing in each of the sentences below. Choose the best answer to complete each sentence.

1. The main ------ of the system is the high operation costs.
   - (A) advantage
   - (B) benefit
   - (C) drawback
   - (D) highlight

2. After several negative comments about the project, the researchers became ------.
   - (A) converted
   - (B) discouraged
   - (C) delighted
   - (D) motivated

3. The large ------ will pay for itself in about 10 years.
   - (A) disaster
   - (B) hazard
   - (C) investment
   - (D) lifespan

4. Over time, renewable energy technologies will continue to ------.
   - (A) assemble
   - (B) evolve
   - (C) rot
   - (D) spawn

5. The scholar has a(n) ------ of knowledge about the subject.
   - (A) abundance
   - (B) adequate
   - (C) technology
   - (D) prominence

Part 6: Text Completion

Four words are missing in the text. Choose the best answers to complete the text.

THE FIRST HYDROELECTRIC POWER PLANT

In 1878, the first hydroelectric power system was built by William Armstrong, a well-known scientist and inventor. He built the system to ------- electricity to run a
                                                                                            1.
single lamp in the art gallery of his country house in Northumberland, England. Although small in scale, this system was an indicator of things to come.

H. J. Rogers, the president of a paper company and a gas light company, learned of Thomas Edison's steam-driven power plant in New York City and was inspired to make a water-powered power plant on the Fox River in Appleton, Wisconsin. He ------- other local business to start a new company with him called the Appleton
    2.
Edison Light Company. A generator was installed and wires connected his home and two paper mills. After a few problems and delays, the hydroelectric power plant began operations on September 30, 1882 with an output of 12.5 kilowatts. The local newspaper reporters said the lamps were as "bright as day."

Naturally, people were very interested in having access to ------- electrical power.
                                                            3.
In fact, the power was so inexpensive that customers paid by the day, not by how much power they used. Some people left their lamps on all the time! All around the world, hydroelectric power stations were built. By 1886, there were more than 45 stations built in the United States and Canada. The popularity of hydroelectric power plants continued to grow and by 1889 there were more than 200 in the United States. Of course, as technology continue to evolve, electricity became available around the world. Today, most people consider electricity to be a ------- of
                                                                                    4.
life, and cannot even imagine life without it.

1. (A) control
   (B) generate
   (C) increase
   (D) spread

2. (A) convinced
   (B) demanded
   (C) followed
   (D) instructed

3. (A) affordable
   (B) delightful
   (C) mysterious
   (D) powerful

4. (A) fact
   (B) luxury
   (C) necessity
   (D) reality

Part 7: Reading Comprehension

Read the advertisement followed by four questions. Choose the best answer to each question.

WINDPOWER 400-WATT WIND TURBINE

This portable wind turbine is the ideal solution for charging your 12-volt batteries. The WINDPOWER 400-watt WIND TURBINE has a weatherproof design which makes it perfect for both land and marine applications. The patented turbine controller system, Optimal Power Tracking Integrated Management Usage System (OPTIMUS) ensures that the turbine shuts down when the batteries are fully charged. $499 MSRP

- perfect for a variety of applications! cottages, camping vehicles, remote power, backup power etc.
- easy to install
- OPTIMUS controller system
- marine-grade coating
- 100% weatherproof
- lightweight aluminum generator body
- 3 high-quality carbon fiber blades
- 2-year limited warranty

NOTE: mounting hardware and tower kits are sold separately.

1. Where is this text likely to be found?
   (A) A science journal
   (B) A shopping catalogue
   (C) A textbook
   (D) An encyclopedia

2. Which of the following is true?
   (A) It has a carbon fiber body.
   (B) It has a common controller system.
   (C) It has a lifetime warranty.
   (D) It has a limited warranty.

3. Who is this product intended for?
   (A) Astronauts
   (B) Campers
   (C) Farmers
   (D) Scientists

4. What does OPTIMUS do?
   (A) Controls the turbine
   (B) Installs the turbine
   (C) Starts the turbine
   (D) Stops the turbine

Our World Today
An Introduction to Environmental Issues

Copyright© 2019
by
Adam Murray
Anderson Passos

All Rights Reserved.
No part of this publication may be reproduced or transmitted in any form or by any means without permission from the authors and Nan'un-do Co., Ltd.

著作権法上，無断複写・複製は禁じられています。

Our World Today: An Introduction to Environmental Issues
英語で考えよう！ 地球の未来 ― クリティカル・シンキングを養う総合英語 ― [B-890]

第 1 刷	2019年4月1日	
第 5 刷	2024年9月1日	
著　者	マレー・アダム	Adam Murray
	パッソス・アンデルソン	Anderson Passos
発行者	南雲一範　Kazunori Nagumo	
発行所	株式会社　南雲堂	
	〒162-0801　東京都新宿区山吹町361	
	NAN'UN-DO Co., Ltd.	
	361 Yamabuki-cho, Shinjuku-ku, Tokyo 162-0801, Japan	
	振替口座：00160-0-46863	
	TEL：03-3268-2311（営業部：学校関係）	
	03-3268-2384（営業部：書店関係）	
	03-3268-2387（編集部）	
	FAX：03-3269-2486	
編集者	丸小雅臣／伊藤宏実	
表　紙	NONdesign	
組　版	Office haru	
検　印	省　略	
コード	ISBN978-4-523-17890-3 C0082	

Printed in Japan

E-mail　nanundo@post.email.ne.jp
URL　https://www.nanun-do.co.jp/